Alphabet

This book has been designed to let young children have lots of fun as they learn the letters of the alphabet. Its easy-to-follow format provides teachers with an endless supply of creative activities that are easy to administer and exciting for children to do.

Each letter of the alphabet is featured on its own page. At the top of each page are activities to do with the children to reinforce letter recognition. Give the children the bottom half of the page to complete independently. When the children have completed all the pages, they can assemble them into a book. Make a copy of page 30 for each child. Have the children decorate the page to create front and back covers for their alphabet book. Staple the books down the left-hand side. The children should use it for review or to take home to share with their family.

Pages 2 and 3 are filled with a variety of exciting activities children can do using any or all of the letters of the alphabet. These activities provide children with hands-on practice with the letters.

The last two pages of this book are review pages that contain activities involving all the letters of the alphabet. They are an important part of helping children tie together the alphabet in its entirety.

As you and the children progress through this book and the alphabet, be sure to point out the letters and their sounds as they appear in various aspects of day-to-day activities. This helps children understand the role of letters and words in their lives and helps broaden their vocabulary. It is hoped that this book will help young children everywhere develop a wider vocabulary and a deeper love of reading.

Activities to Use With the Alphabet

Block Letters
Using building blocks from the classroom, have the children build two- and three-dimensional letters.

Alphabet Musical Chairs
Have each child tape a square of construction paper to a chair. On each square, write a letter of the alphabet. Begin playing musical chairs. When the music stops, have each child call out the letter that he or she sat on. Continue to play until all the chairs and letters have been called.

Pantomime Letters
Have the children pretend to be a specific letter from the alphabet. Let the children not in the pantomime guess what letter is being pantomimed.

Clay Letters
Make a dough mixture from salt, flour, and water. Roll the dough in coils and have the children mold the letters of the alphabet. Bake the letters on a cookie sheet on low heat for several hours. Have the children paint their letters using exotic colors and designs. Display the letters around the classroom.

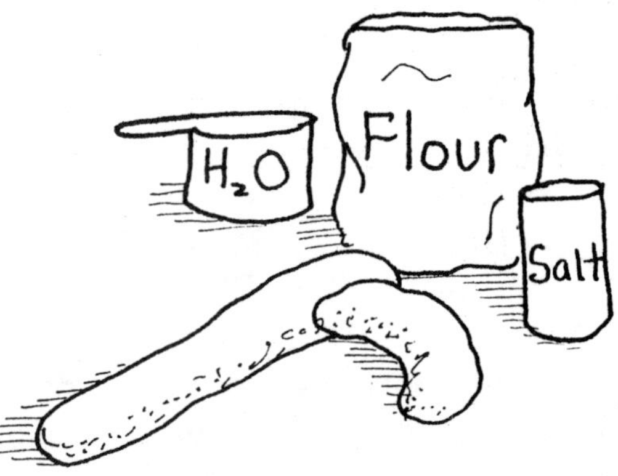

Red Rover Alphabet
Pin a letter from the alphabet on each child. Play "Red Rover" with the children calling a child over by yelling out the letter attached to him or her.

Object Pass
Have a pile of objects available. Have the children sit in a circle. Start some music and pass an object around the circle. When the music stops, have the child holding the object call out the letter sound that the object begins with. Continue the music using a different object each time.

Hat Pull
In a large top hat, place construction paper squares that each contain a letter of the alphabet. Have the children take turns pulling a letter from the hat. The children then think of three words that begin with the letter sound.

Activities continued

Crayon Shaving Letters
Have the children place crayon shavings on a sheet of wax paper. Be certain to have the children place the shavings in a letter form. Cover the shavings with another sheet of wax paper. Using a warm iron, melt the crayon shavings by ironing over wax paper. Let the wax paper cool. Peel the wax paper off the crayon. Have the children share the crayon letters.

Marble Alphabet
Tape a large circle of masking tape onto the floor. Tape construction paper circles inside the large circle. On each circle, write a different letter. Have the children take turns rolling marbles into the circle and calling out the letter that their marble lands on.

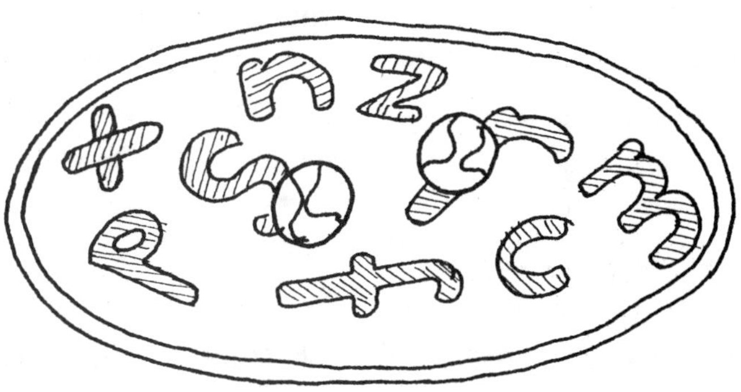

Letter Bags
Choose several letters to reinforce. Label one paper bag for each chosen letter. Gather five objects that begin with each letter. Lay the objects randomly on the floor. Have the children take turns choosing an object and putting it in the correct bag.

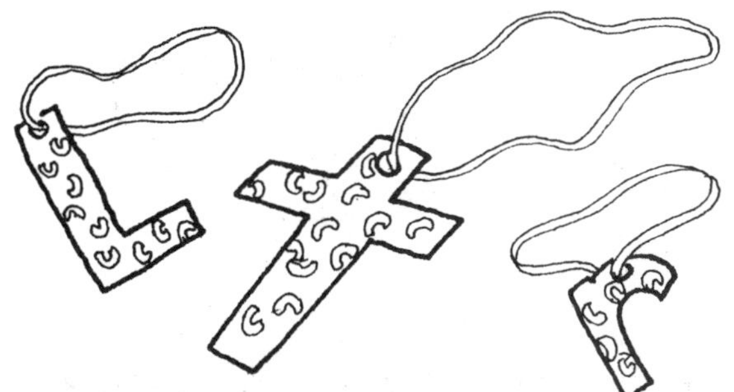

Alphabet Necklaces
Cut letters out of posterboard. Give each child a letter. Have him or her decorate it using makers. Let the children glue macaroni on it. They can then punch a hole in their letter, tie a piece of string through it, and wear it.

Shaving Cream Letters
Place a small amount of shaving cream on a tabletop. Let each child practice making letters in the shaving cream using his or her fingertips.

Letter Mobiles
Assign each child a letter. Have him or her find five pictures that begin with the letter and glue them to construction paper. After the children cut out their pictures from the construction paper, have them cut a hole in them, and thread each with a piece of yarn. The children can tie the pictures to a coat hanger and present them to the class.

Letter Practice
Have the children practice their uppercase and lowercase **A**'s by finger writing in the air. Explain that *air* begins with the letter **A**. Ask the children to think of other words that begin with the same letter.

The A Hunt
Have the children go around the room looking for letter **A**'s on anything they can find.

The A Grab Bag
Fill a large paper bag with items that begin with the letter **A**. Have the children choose items from the bag and identify them by name.

Dried Apples
Explain that *apple* begins with the letter **A**. Have the children peel and core apples. Cut the apples into thin slices and lay them on a piece of screen. After several days, let the children taste the dried apples.

Snack Ideas
apple slices, alfalfa sprouts, apricots, avocado slices

Name the picture words below.
Color the ones that begin like *apple*.

A a A a

Aa•Bb•Cc•Dd•Ee•Ff•Gg•Hh•Ii•Jj•Kk•Ll•Mm•Nn•Oo•Pp•Qq•Rr•Ss•Tt•Uu•Vv•Ww•Xx•Yy•Zz

Letter Practice

Give each child a black sheet of construction paper. Using chalk, have the children draw an uppercase and lowercase **B** on their paper. Finally, have the children glue brightly colored buttons on the chalk lines to form the letters. Explain that *black, bright,* and *buttons* start with the letter **B.**

Ball Sorting

Fill a large laundry basket with balls. Include a basketball, beach ball, baseball, tennis ball, and football. Explain that *ball* begins with the letter **B**. Have the children identify each type of ball and recognize those which begin with the letter **B**.

Bottle Bowling

Collect six, empty, two-liter plastic soda bottles. Fill the bottles with an inch of sand. Arrange the bottles in a V shape and have the children take turns rolling a blue ball into the bottles. Explain that *blue*, *ball*, *bottle*, and *bowling* all start with the letter **B**.

Body B's

Have pairs of children practice making the lowercase **b** using their bodies. Trace the letter with your hand to help the children visualize the lowercase **b**.

Bubbles

Write the word *bubble* on a sheet of graph paper. Have the children circle the **B**'s in the word. Fill a water table or sink with bubbles and let the children have some fun!

Snack Ideas

Banana Barges—To make these, give each child a banana cut lengthwise. Let the children sprinkle bits of brickle or beernuts on top.

Color the balloons that have objects that begin with a **b**.

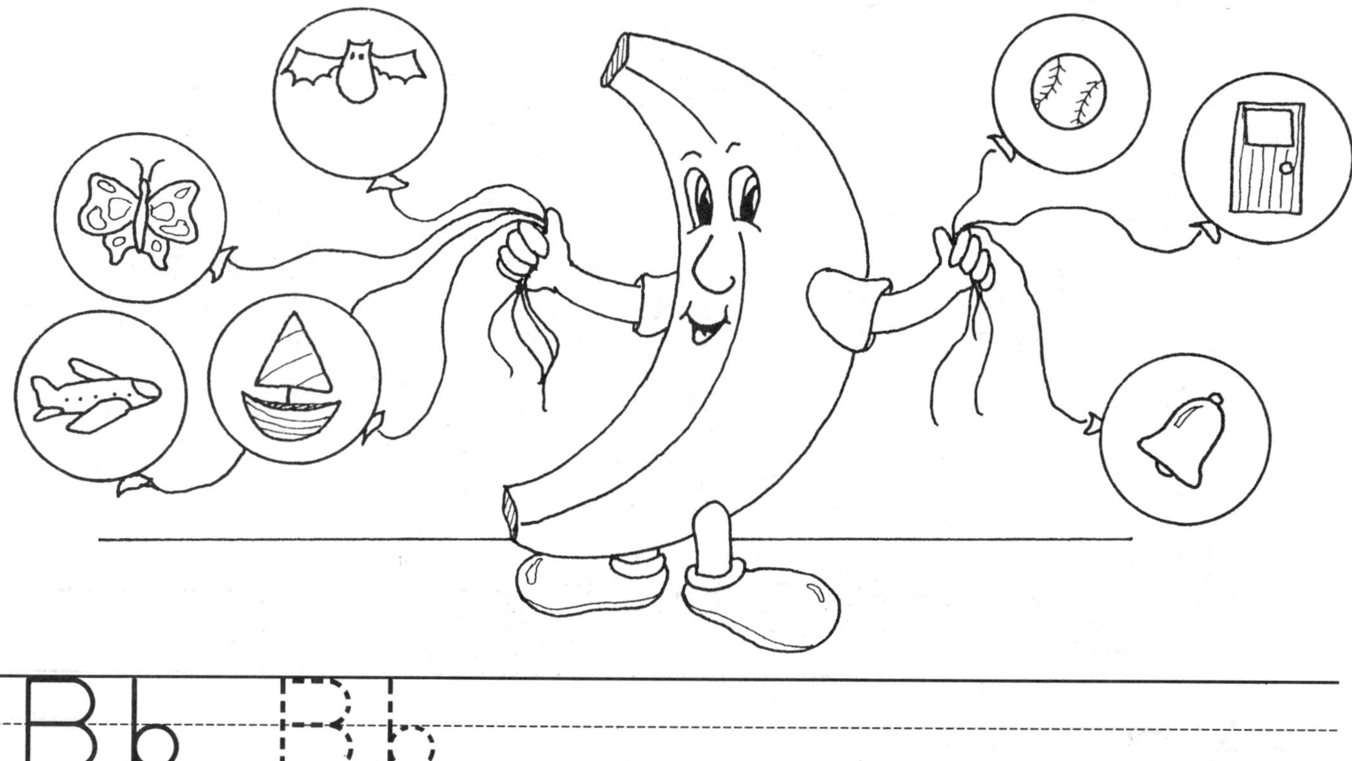

Bb Bb

Letter Practice

Give each child a sheet of paper. Have the children put crayon shavings in the shape of an uppercase and lowercase **C**. Cover the paper with wax paper. Use a warm iron to melt the crayon shavings. Remove the wax paper and expose the colorful letters. Explain how *crayons* and *color* begin with the letter **C**.

Crazy Cutlery Creatures

Give the children plastic cutlery and explain that they are going to turn the cutlery into crazy creatures. Write the title of the activity on the chalkboard and have the children recognize the **C**'s in the title. Give the children glue, scraps of paper, fabric, pompons, yarn, buttons, and any other decorating materials they can use to create their creatures.

Colorful Cups

Before serving cranberry juice for a snack, have the children color paper cups with things that begin with the letter **C**. Provide them with brightly colored markers they can use. Explain that *cranberry*, *colorful*, and *cup* all begin with the letter **C**.

Snack Ideas

cookies, crackers, carrots, cupcakes, cantaloupe, corn bread, cranberry juice

---

Circle each picture that begins with **C**.

C c C c

Dd

Aa•Bb•Cc•Dd•Ee•Ff•Gg•Hh•Ii•Jj•Kk•Ll•Mm•Nn•Oo•Pp•Qq•Rr•Ss•Tt•Uu•Vv•Ww•Xx•Yy•Zz

Letter Practice
Mix one cup of salt with one cup of flour and a tablespoon of powdered alum. Mix the ingredients with water until they have the consistency of putty. Give each child a portion of the dough. Have the children form the dough into uppercase and lowercase **D**'s. Explain that *dough* begins with the letter **D**.

Do the Dinosaur Dance
After reading about dinosaurs, have the children discuss different types of dinosaurs. Ask the children to think about a kind of dinosaur they would like to be. Play some music and have the children do a dinosaur dance. Explain that *dance* and *dinosaur* begin with the letter **D**.

Dinosaur-Egg Hunt
Decorate a rubber ball with different shapes and colors. Have the children pretend that it is a dinosaur's egg. While the children close their eyes, hide the ball. Leave a trail of paper **D**'s (uppercase and lowercase) around the classroom leading to the hidden egg. Send the children on the Dinosaur-Egg Hunt.

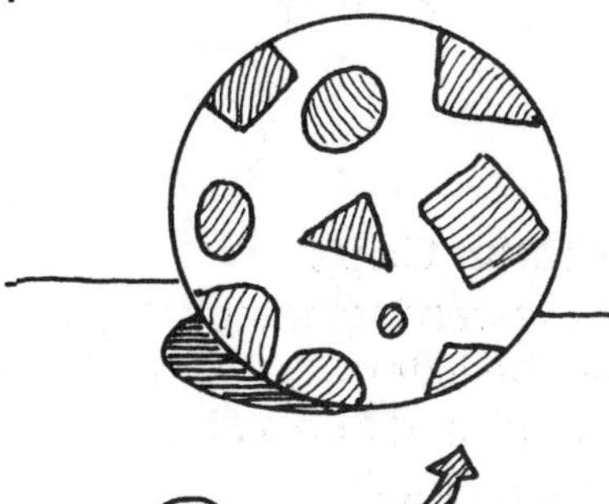

Snack Idea
doughnut holes

Color all the objects that begin with **D**.

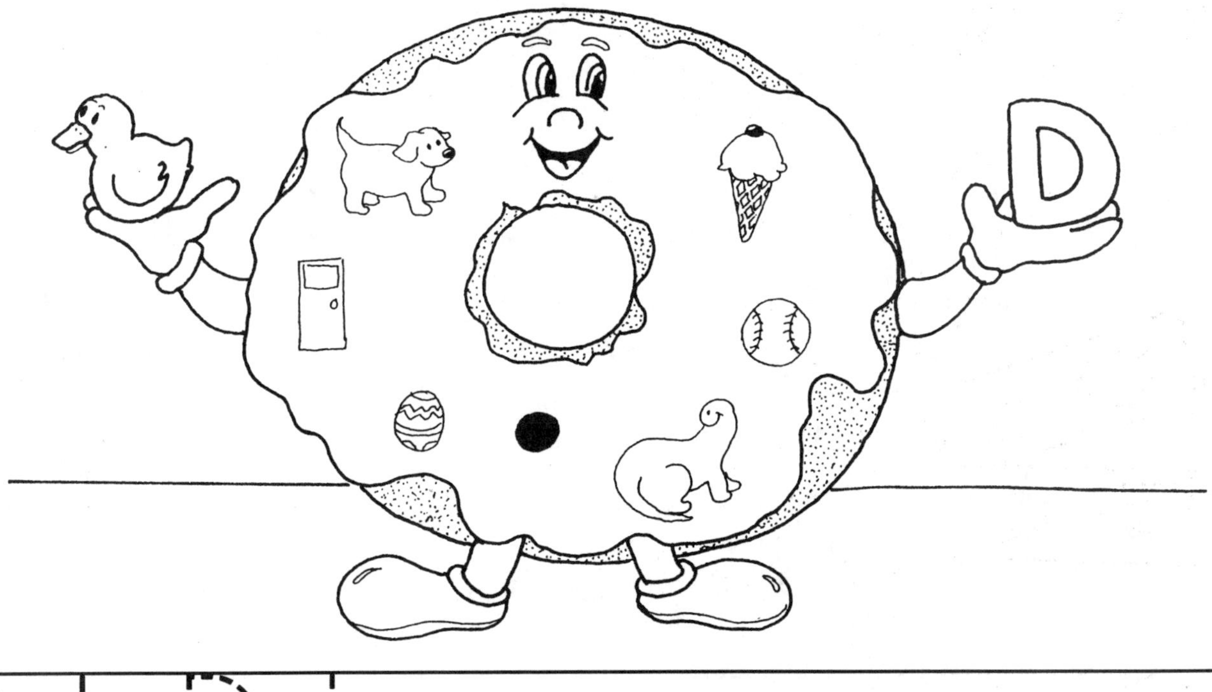

Dd Dd

Aa•Bb•Cc•Dd•Ee•Ff•Gg•Hh•Ii•Jj•Kk•Ll•Mm•Nn•Oo•Pp•Qq•Rr•Ss•Tt•Uu•Vv•Ww•Xx•Yy•Zz

Letter Practice

On a sheet of paper, have the children glue pieces of emery boards into the shapes of the uppercase and lowercase **E**'s. Display the emery board **E**'s around the classroom.

Eggheads

Display an enlarged picture of Evan the Egg in the classroom. Tell the children that they are going to help Evan grow some hair. Give each child an egg carton section with half of an eggshell in it. Have each child draw a face on his or her egg using markers. Help the children fill their eggshells with soil. Finally, have them plant some grass seeds in their eggshell. Water the eggs and place them in a sunny area. Eventually, the eggs will sprout green grass hair. Throughout the process, remind the children that *Evan* and *egg* begin with the letter **E**.

Eggplant Examination

Buy a couple of eggplants at the grocery store. Cut them up in different ways. Talk to the children about the different characteristics of the eggplant. Explain that the process of cutting and looking for characteristics is called *examination*. Remind the children that *eggplant* and *examination* are words that begin with the letter **E**.

Snack Ideas

egg salad sandwiches, eggplant

Circle all the objects that begin with **E**.

E e

Aa•Bb•Cc•Dd•Ee•Ff•Gg•Hh•Ii•Jj•Kk•Ll•Mm•Nn•Oo•Pp•Qq•Rr•Ss•Tt•Uu•Vv•Ww•Xx•Yy•Zz

Letter Practice

Give each child two strands of dental floss, scissors, and glue. Instruct the children to form the uppercase and lowercase **F**'s using their floss. Have them glue their floss **F**'s onto a piece of construction paper.

Finger Fossils

Talk to the children about fossils. Explain that *fossils* and *fingers* begin with the letter **F**. Cut a small milk carton in half for each child. Pour plaster of Paris into each carton. As the plaster of Paris begins to harden, have each child make a fossil print of his or her fingers. Once the plaster of Paris has completely hardened, have the children remove the carton from their fossil. Have them practice writing the uppercase and lowercase **F**'s around the sides of the fossil.

Fishing Fun

Using old magazines, have the children cut out pictures of things that begin with the letter **F**. They can then glue these pictures onto posterboard and cut them out. Fasten a paper clip to each picture. Next, make a fishing rod. To do this, tie a magnet to one end of a piece of string. Tie the other end of the string to a yardstick. Then, let the children go fishing! When the magnet on the string touches one of the paper clips attached to one of the pictures, the child will have caught an item that begins with the letter **F**. Have each child tell what he or she caught.

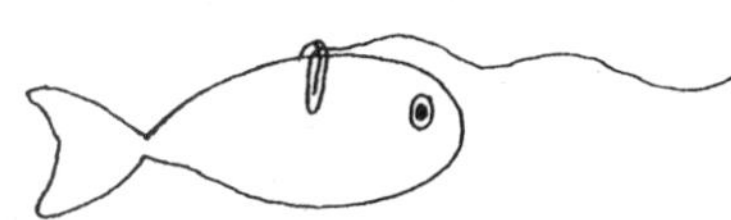

Snack Ideas

Frogs on a Log—The logs are stalks of celery filled with peanut butter. The frogs are raisins that are placed on the peanut butter. Frozen fruit on a stick or fish shaped crackers are other snack ideas.

Draw a line from the objects that begin with **F** to the **Ff**.

Ff

Aa • Bb • Cc • Dd • Ee • Ff • Gg • Hh • Ii • Jj • Kk • Ll • Mm • Nn • Oo • Pp • Qq • Rr • Ss • Tt • Uu • Vv • Ww • Xx • Yy • Zz

Letter Practice

Give each child a glue bottle, some glitter, and a sheet of construction paper. Tell the children to practice making uppercase and lowercase **G**'s on their paper by pouring glue in the letter forms. Have the children decorate their **G**'s by sprinkling glitter on the glue. Explain that *glitter* and *glue* both start with the letter **G**.

Gumball Graph

5						
4						
3						
2						
1						
	Red	Blue	Yellow	Orange	Green	Pink

Gumball Graphs

Label a graph with colors along the bottom and numbers along the side. (See diagram.) Place a bag of gumballs on a tray. Have the children help count how many of each color of gumball is available. Graph the results together. Explain that *gumball* and *graph* begin with the letter **G**.

All-Purpose Gift-Giving Paper

Talk about gift-giving and how one prepares a gift for giving. Explain that *gift* and *giving* begin with the letter **G**. Give each child a strip of white butcher paper and markers. Have the children decorate the paper with as many uppercase and lowercase **G**'s as they can. Instruct the children to make different sizes and colors of **G**'s. Remind them to turn their papers around and write some letters upside down. Encourage the children to use their decorative paper for gift-giving.

Snack Ideas

green grapes, granola, gumballs, grape juice

Color the lowercase **g**'s purple.
Color the uppercase **G**'s red.

G g g g g G g G G G G g g G g

G g G g

Aa•Bb•Cc•Dd•Ee•Ff•Gg•Hh•Ii•Jj•Kk•Ll•Mm•Nn•Oo•Pp•Qq•Rr•Ss•Tt•Uu•Vv•Ww•Xx•Yy•Zz

Letter Practice

Make heart-shaped cutouts for the children. Have them glue the heart shapes into uppercase and lowercase **H** forms on a piece of paper.

H Hopscotch

Cut out pictures or draw pictures of a hand, a heart, a hat, a hammer, a hose, a hamburger, and a house. Draw a hopscotch grid and tape or draw one of the pictures listed above in each square. Have the children take turns tossing beanbags into the square and calling out the **H** words as they retrieve the beanbag.

The Hula-Hoop Hop

Review the letters A-H using the Hula-Hoop Hop. Place eight Hula-Hoops apart from one another in hopping distance. With chalk, draw one letter (uppercase and lowercase) from A-H in each Hula-Hoop. Be sure to place them in correct sequence. Have the children take turns hopping through the Hula-Hoops and reciting the alphabet to the letter **H**.

Hair Hats

Ask the children to talk about different kinds of hair. Ask them what kind of hair they would most like to have. Then, tell them that they are going to have a chance to make a hat that gives them the head of hair they have always wanted. Form a cone hat out of construction paper for each child. Instruct the children to write uppercase and lowercase **H**'s on their cones with crayons. Supply the children with various colors of yarn. Have them cut lengths of yarn to match the length of hair they would like to have. Using masking tape, help the children tape the strands of yarn to the inside of the cone.

Snack Ideas

honey-dipped apple slices, hot chocolate

Color the pictures that begin with **H** red.

Hh Hh

Letter Practice

Give each child a handful of ice chips. Tell the children to form the uppercase and lowercase **I**'s out of the ice. If this activity cannot be done outside, place the ice chips in a contained area. Let the children enjoy the melting process.

Islands in the Sandbox

Fill a water table with water. Talk to the children about islands. Explain that *island* begins with the letter **I**. Explain that an island is completely surrounded by water. Show the children how to make an island in the water table by pouring a mound of sand in the middle of the table. Pour the sand in the shape of an **I**. Tell the children that you have created an I-shaped island. Encourage the children to try to make their own islands.

Ice Cube Igloos

Talk to the children about Eskimos and the function of an igloo. Show the children pictures of igloos. Have the children try to make an igloo of their own using ice cubes. Be sure to do this activity outdoors or in a contained area where water spills would not be a problem.

Ink Art

Give each child a pen. Have the children watch you open and examine a pen internally. Identify the ink well. Give each child a piece of paper. Have them make an ink drawing. Caution the children about ink spills and marks.

Snack Ideas

ice cream, frozen ice drinks

Find the hidden **I**'s.

Color them.

How many did you find? __________

Ii Ii

Aa • Bb • Cc • Dd • Ee • Ff • Gg • Hh • Ii • Jj • Kk • Ll • Mm • Nn • Oo • Pp • Qq • Rr • Ss • Tt • Uu • Vv • Ww • Xx • Yy • Zz

Letter Practice

On a piece of paper, have the children glue jellybeans in the shape of an uppercase and lowercase **J**.

The Job Jar

Have the children brainstorm as many jobs for the classroom as there are students in the class. Write each job on a small piece of paper and place it in a jar labeled "Job Jar." At certain times during the week, have each child reach in the jar to remove a job paper. Tell the children that they are responsible for completing the job they selected.

Jell-O Jigglers

Prepare a large box of Jell-O jigglers mix. Using plastic knives, have the children cut **J**'s out of the hardened Jell-O.

June and January Differences

On a sheet of butcher paper, write *June* and *January*. Talk about the weather during these months and point out the **J**'s in the words. Have the children draw pictures of things they would do outdoors during June and January.

Juice, Juice, Juice

Write the word *juice* on the chalkboard and have the children notice the **J**. Talk about different fruit and vegetable juices that are available. Show the children how to squeeze juice from oranges using a hand juicer. Collect the juice and serve it for a snack.

Snack Ideas

Jell-O, juice, jellybeans, jam on toast

Write a **j** or a **J** in each jar.

J j J j

Aa•Bb•Cc•Dd•Ee•Ff•Gg•Hh•Ii•Jj•Kk•Ll•Mm•Nn•Oo•Pp•Qq•Rr•Ss•Tt•Uu•Vv•Ww•Xx•Yy•Zz

Letter Practice

Have the children form uppercase and lowercase **K**'s out of kite string. Have them glue the string letters on a sheet of paper.

Crazy K Sentences

Have the children finish the following **K** sentences:

Kelly the kitten ate a whole ________.
I dropped the key into a kettle of ________.
Kaitie's kite blew into ________.
If I were a King, my Kingdom would ________.
A kiss from a kangaroo could give you ________.
Kevin kicked the ________.

Kings of the Kitchen

Set up a kitchen in a dramatic play area. Assign groups of children different responsibilities in the kitchen. Have one group plan a meal, one group cook the meal, one group serve the meal, and one group clean up after the meal.

Kazoo Madness

Try to collect several kazoos and have the children form a parade. Place masking tape in the shape of a large **K** on the floor. Have the children take turns marching along the **K** while playing their kazoos.

Kitten Kindness

Arrange for a visit to or from the local Humane Society. Focus on caring for kittens. Read *One Little Kitten* by Tana Hoban to reinforce the letter **K**.

Snack Idea

Have the children make their own kabobs. Have cheese cubes, cocktail wieners, pickles, celery, or fruit available for spearing.

Color all the pictures that begin with **K**.
Find the path.

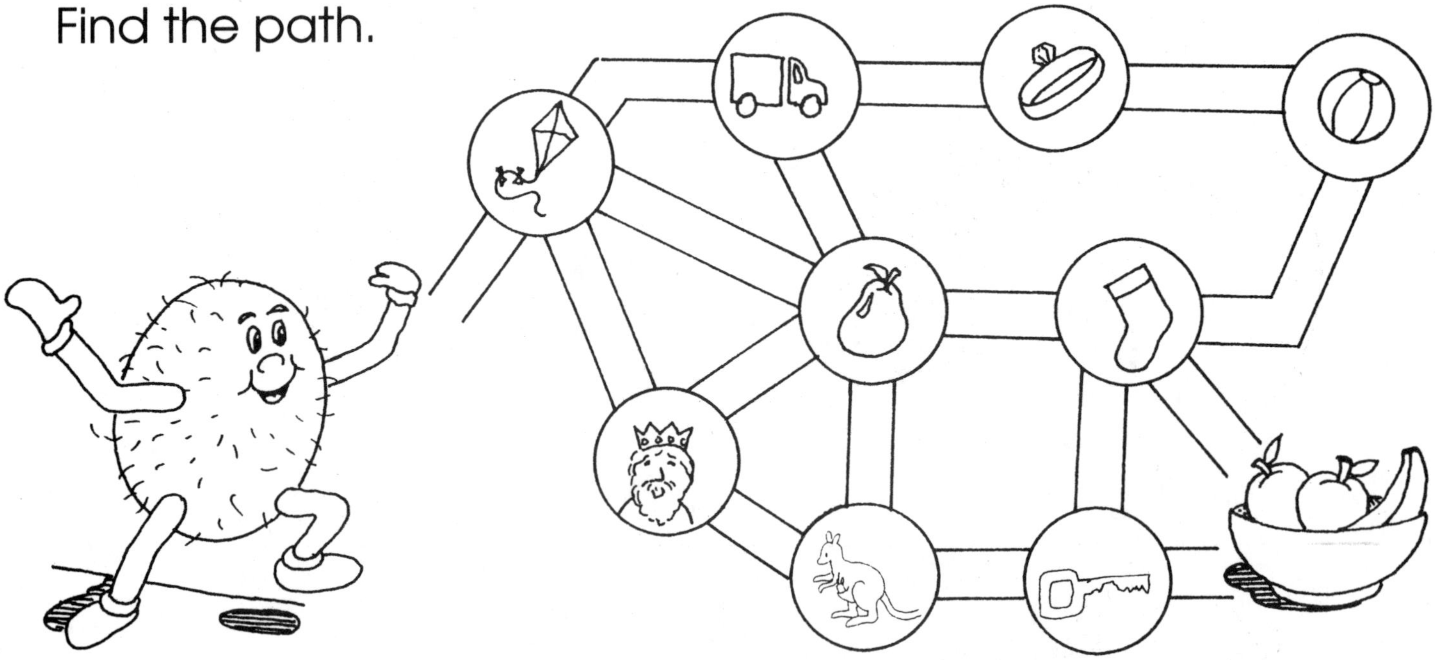

Kk Kk

Aa•Bb•Cc•Dd•Ee•Ff•Gg•Hh•Ii•Jj•Kk•Ll•Mm•Nn•Oo•Pp•Qq•Rr•Ss•Tt•Uu•Vv•Ww•Xx•Yy•Zz

Letter Practice

Give each child a sheet of paper. Have the children practice writing uppercase and lowercase **L**'s using lipstick. Explain that *lipstick* begins with the letter **L**.

Lego Letters

Tell the children that they are going to have letter practice time. Explain that they will be using Lego blocks to form the letters. Begin by helping the children make uppercase and lowercase **L**'s like those in the words *Lego* and *letter.*

Lollipop Letter L's

Give each child a construction paper circle. Instruct the children to practice writing uppercase and lowercase **L**'s on the circle. Then give each child a tongue depressor. Have the children glue their circles to the tongue depressors to create a lollipop. Explain that *lollipop* and *letters* begin with the letter **L**.

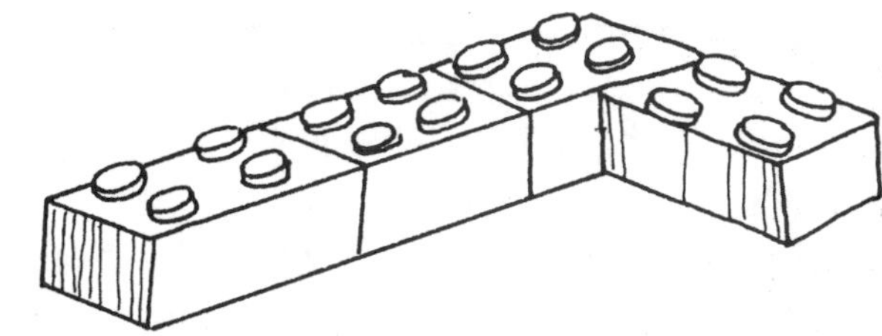

Lunch Box Label

Give each child an adhesive label. Explain to the children that they are going to make a label for their lunch box. Help the children discover the letter **L** in *lunch box* and *label.* Provide markers the children can use to decorate the labels. Have the children stick their labels to their lunch boxes.

Snack Ideas

lemonade, licorice, lasagna, lettuce, lemon-lime popsicles

Circle all the pictures that begin with **L**.

Letter Practice

Give each child a sheet of paper, a bottle of glue, and a handful of M&M's. Have the children glue their M&M's to their paper in the shape of an uppercase and lowercase **M**.

Messy Mirrors

Make a bowl of mud by adding a little water to some topsoil. Mix it together well. Give each child a small mirror. Instruct the children to practice making uppercase and lowercase **M**'s on their mirror using mud. Reinforce that *mud* and *mirror* start with the letter **M**.

Maraca Music

Explain what a maraca is to the children. Have each child fill a small yogurt container with beads or popcorn. Help the children seal their containers to form a maraca. Have the children make music with their maracas. Ask them to listen to the different sounds each maraca makes.

Magic M's

Give each child a white crayon, a white sheet of paper, a paintbrush, and a cup of diluted water color paint. Have the children practice writing the lower and uppercase **M**'s on their paper using a white crayon. Have the children watch the mystery **M**'s appear as they paint over their papers using diluted watercolor paint.

Minnow Mischief

Fill a large water table with water. Obtain some minnows from a local pet store or nearby lake. Let the children observe the minnows noting their speed, color, size, and number.

Snack Ideas

milk shakes, marshmallow treats, milk, melons, macaroni

Match the lowercase **m**'s to the uppercase **M**'s.

Nn

Aa • Bb • Cc • Dd • Ee • Ff • Gg • Hh • Ii • Jj • Kk • Ll • Mm • Nn • Oo • Pp • Qq • Rr • Ss • Tt • Uu • Vv • Ww • Xx • Yy • Zz

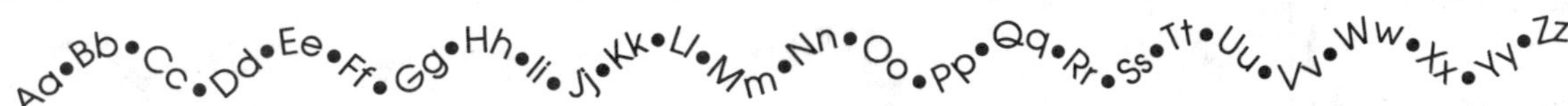

Letter Practice
Have the children cut up newspapers into tiny pieces. Have each child practice making uppercase and lowercase **N**'s by gluing the newspaper scraps onto the paper in the form of the letters.

Noodle Necklaces
Collect a number of different types of noodles. Have the children string a necklace of noodles. A construction paper letter **N** could be glued on a center noodle as a pendant. Explain to the children that *noodle* and *necklace* begin with the letter **N**.

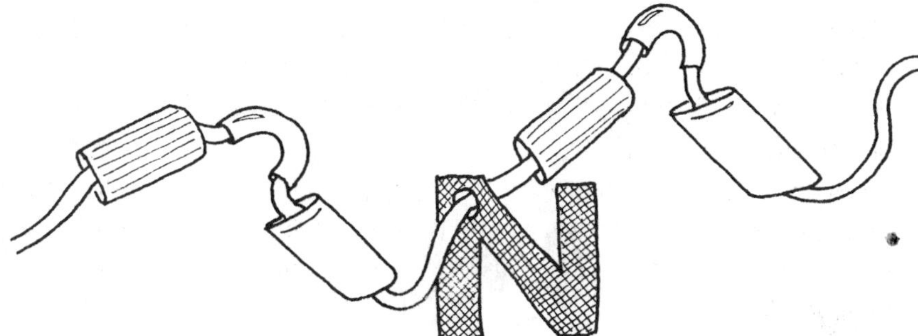

Nut Mix
Place a large group of nuts on a tray.
Have the children name each nut. Write the names on the chalkboard. Circle all the nuts that have the letter **N** in them. Be sure to include hazelnuts, walnuts, peanuts, and acorns.

News
Ask each child to bring in a news clipping. Talk about each story and its relevance.

Snack Ideas
nuts, noodles, nachos

Write the letter **n** beside each picture that begins with **n**.

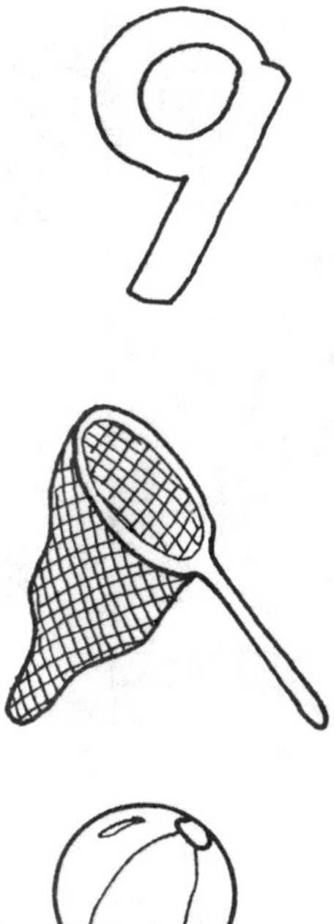

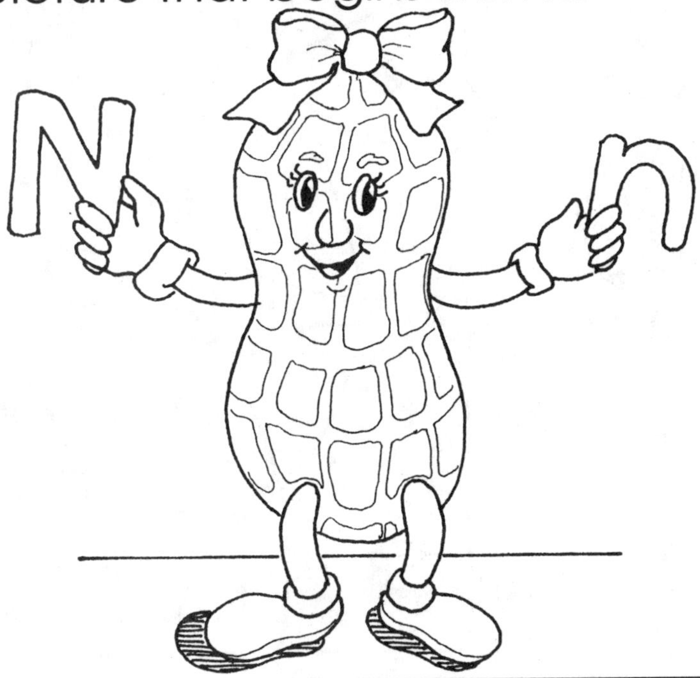

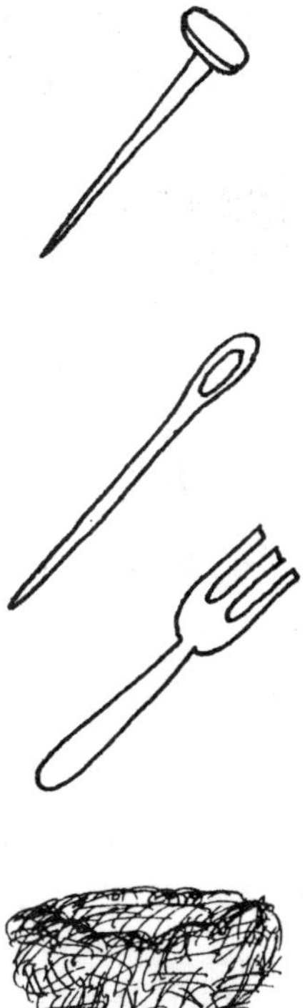

Nn Nn

Letter Practice
Give each child a paintbrush and some orange paint. Have the children paint orange uppercase and lowercase **O**'s on a sheet of paper. Explain that *orange* beings with the letter **O**.

Oliver's Opposites
Tell the children that they are going to take turns pretending to be Oliver. Oliver will call out a word and his friends must say the opposite of that word. A list to work from might include big/small, high/low, stand/sit, walk/run, soft/hard, straight/crooked, happy/sad, or smile/frown.

The Oval Octopus
Show the children how an octopus can be drawn using ovals. Use the illustration to the left as a guide. Have the children draw their own oval octopus. Explain that *oval* and *octopus* begin with the letter **O**.

Snack Ideas
orange slices, olives

Color the **B** spaces blue.
Color the **O** spaces red.

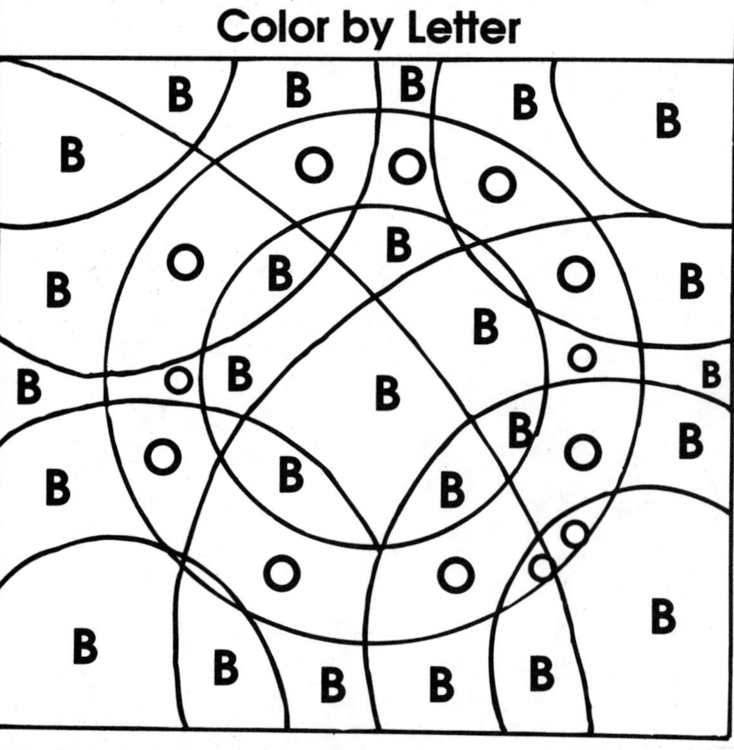

Aa•Bb•Cc•Dd•Ee•Ff•Gg•Hh•Ii•Jj•Kk•Ll•Mm•Nn•Oo•Pp•Qq•Rr•Ss•Tt•Uu•Vv•Ww•Xx•Yy•Zz

Letter Practice

Give each child a sheet of purple construction paper and a few pipe cleaners. Have the children form uppercase and lowercase **P**'s out of the pipe cleaners. Tell them to glue their pipe cleaner **P**'s to their purple papers. Remind the children that *purple*, *pipe cleaner*, and *paper* begin with the letter **P**.

Pea Words in the Pod

Cover a bulletin board with a solid color of paper. Title the bulletin board "Word Pod." Cut out a pea pod and eight circles from green construction paper. Have the children help discover words that begin with the letter **P**. Write a **P** word on each circle. Tape the circles to the pea pod on the bulletin board. Review the words throughout the week.

Pizza P's

Have the children make a quick mix pizza dough. Give each child a ball of dough. Tell the children to roll and form their dough into a letter **P**. Next, the children can place sauce, peppers, and pepperoni on their pizza **P**'s. Bake and serve the pizza **P**'s for a snack.

Potato Print P's

Cut a potato in half. Carve a reverse image (lowercase letter b) of the letter **P** onto each potato half. Give each child a sheet of pink paper, a half of a carved potato, and a small plate of purple paint. Have the children dip their potatoes in purple paint and print them on their pink paper. Encourage the children to fill their papers with **P**'s.

Snack Ideas

pineapple pieces, pumpkin seeds, popsicles, pizza

Color the **p**'s yellow.
Color the **b**'s orange.
Color the **d**'s gray.

Letter Practice

Give each child some Q-Tips, a sheet of paper, and some glue. Have the children glue their Q-Tips in the form of an uppercase and lowercase **Q** on their paper.

The Alphabet Quilt

Provide each child with a pre-cut square of paper that has been labeled with a letter of the alphabet. Explain that a quilt is made by sewing small pieces of fabric together to form a large blanket. Tell the children that they are going to be making a paper quilt of the alphabet. Each child must decorate his or her letter square with items beginning with the letter indicated. Eventually, tape all the squares together adding any additional blank squares to form a complete rectangular shape.

Quick or Quiet Moves

Tell the children that they are going to practice moving in two ways—quickly and quietly. Have each child try a movement quickly and then quietly. Discuss the beginning sounds of *quickly* and *quietly.*

Quarter Rubbings

Give each child a quarter, a crayon, and a piece of paper. Tell the children to write an uppercase and lowercase **Q** on their paper. Then instruct them to use another color of crayon to do quarter rubbings all over their paper.

Snack Ideas

fruit in quarters, milk poured from a quart

Color the milk drops that have objects beginning with the letter **q** on them.

Queen Quart

Letter Practice

Give each child a strip of red ribbon, scissors, glue, and a sheet of paper. Have the children cut their red ribbons to form uppercase and lowercase **R**'s on their paper. Tell the children to glue their ribbons to their paper.

Ruler Relay Races

Depending on the class size, divide the children into four or six groups. Draw two lines on a playing field approximately 20 yards apart. Have the groups form single file lines facing one another. Give the first person in each group behind the same line a ruler. Tell the children that when given the starting signal, they are to run and pass the ruler to the first person in the group facing them. They must then sit down at the end of their line. The first group to have all of its members sitting is the winning group. Remind the children that *ruler, relay, run*, and *race* begin with the letter **R**.

Rectangles With Rulers

Discuss rectangular shapes with the children. Explain the function of a ruler to the children. With a pencil and ruler, have the children practice making rectangular shapes. Finally, have the children color their rectangles red.

Rock Collecting

Take the children outdoors and have them collect rocks. Bring the rocks back to the classroom and have the children examine the rocks. Have the children note similarities in rock sizes, colors, shapes, and textures. Finally, have the children help make large letter **R**'s on the floor using the rocks that they collected.

Snack Ideas

raisins, radishes, rhubarb, raspberries

Color the lowercase **r**'s yellow.
Color the uppercase **R**'s blue.

Rr Rr

Ss

Aa•Bb•Cc•Dd•Ee•Ff•Gg•Hh•Ii•Jj•Kk•Ll•Mm•Nn•Oo•Pp•Qq•Rr•Ss•Tt•Uu•Vv•Ww•Xx•Yy•Zz

Letter Practice

Give each child a square of construction paper, a bottle of glue, some salt, and some sand. Using glue, have the children draw uppercase and lowercase **S**'s on their paper. Have the children pour sand or salt on the glue. Have them shake the excess sand or salt from the paper. For additional fun, have the children color their sand or salt (using chalk dust) before pouring it on the glue letters.

Soap Scribbles

Let the children have some fun while cleaning the classroom. Give the children some small bars of soap. Then, ask them to do the unthinkable—scribble on the windows. Suggest they write words or draw things that begin with the letter **S**. After some creative play, have the children wipe the windows using water and sponges. Point out that *soap, scribbles*, and *sponges* all begin with the letter **S**.

Simon Says, Only With an S

Tell the children that they are going to play "Simon Says." Instead of waiting to hear if Simon "says," the children must wait to hear what Simon would like them to do. If the movement begins with a letter **S**, then they must do the action. If the movement begins with a letter other than **S**, they must remain still.

Snack Ideas

spaghetti, soup, sunflower seeds, sesame snacks

Draw a line from the sock to all the pictures that begin with an **S**.

S s S s

Aa•Bb•Cc•Dd•Ee•Ff•Gg•Hh•Ii•Jj•Kk•Ll•Mm•Nn•Oo•Pp•Qq•Rr•Ss•Tt•Uu•Vv•Ww•Xx•Yy•Zz

Letter Practice

Have the children practice making uppercase and lowercase **T**'s on a piece of paper with a marker. Then, have the children glue toothpicks on their marker lines. Explain that *toothpick* begins with the letter **T**.

T Train

Tell the children that they are going to be a train. In order for the train to move, the children must take turns saying a word that begins with the letter **T**. Children should use a different **T** word each time. The children will follow a leader taking turns calling out **T** words. For each correct word, the train should move forward one step. If a word is incorrect, the train must stay stationary. Focus on the distance the train may go!

Tidy Teeth

Invite a school nurse to talk to the children about good dental hygiene. Have the children bring their toothbrushes and toothpaste to school for after-lunch brushing one day.

Masking Tape T's

Put several masking tape **T**'s, both uppercase and lowercase, on the floor. Have the children pretend they are tightrope walkers as they walk along the masking tape letter **T**.

Snack Ideas

tangerines, toast, tomatoes, tostadas, tuna salad

Color the items that begin with the letter **T**.

Letter Practice
Cut out class photos of all the students. Have the children help glue the photos together in a large form of the letters **U** and **S**. Explain that the word *us* is used to describe the group and begins with the letter **U**.

Up and Under Obstacle Course
Arrange an obstacle course in the classroom for children to climb up, under, and through. Remind the children to call out the action they are doing as they climb up or under.

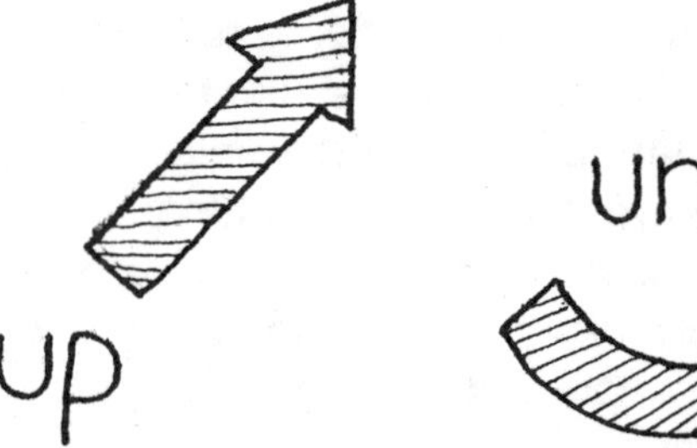

Uniform Dress-Up
Talk to the children about various uniforms our community helpers wear. Put a large box of these kinds of uniforms in the classroom. Allow the children to dress up in the uniforms.

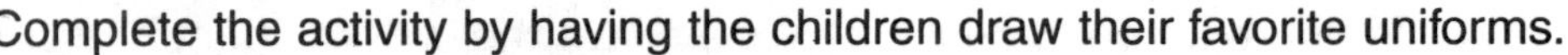

Complete the activity by having the children draw their favorite uniforms.

Undo, Unzip, Uncover, Unbutton
Place the following items at a station in the room: jacket with a zipper, vest with buttons, robe with ties, shovel and pail full of sand with a large shell in the bottom. Have the children explore undoing, unzipping, and unbuttoning. Explain that each of the skills begins with "un."

Snack Ideas
pineapple upside-down cake

Color the letter **U**'s in each cube.

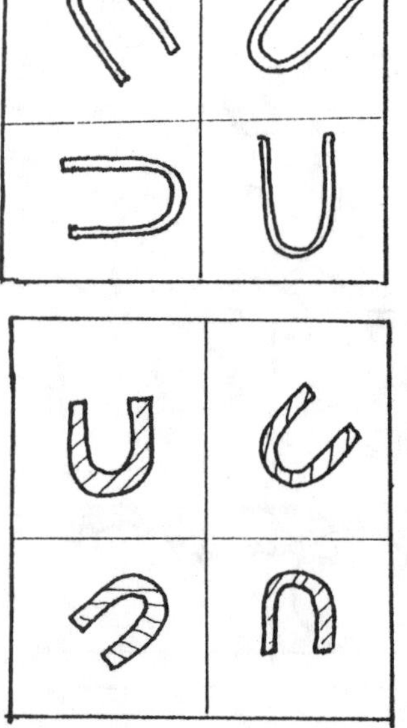

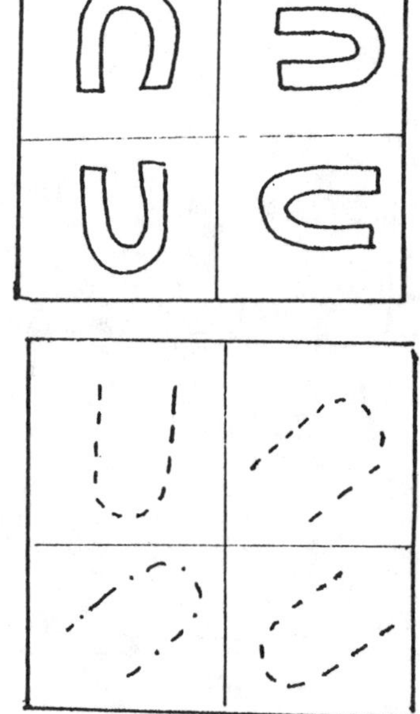

Aa•Bb•Cc•Dd•Ee•Ff•Gg•Hh•Ii•Jj•Kk•Ll•Mm•Nn•Oo•Pp•Qq•Rr•Ss•Tt•Uu•Vv•Ww•Xx•Yy•Zz

Letter Practice

Tell the children that they are going to make vanishing letter **V**'s. Fill a bucket with water. Give each child a paintbrush. Tell the children to dip their paintbrush into the water. Then, have them paint uppercase and lowercase **V**'s on a sidewalk or cement. Tell the children to watch as the **V**'s vanish when the sun heats the ground.

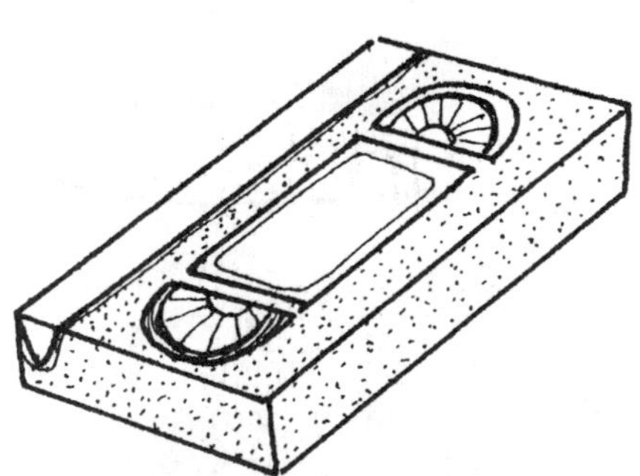

Veterinarian Visit

Arrange a visit to a local veterinarian clinic or have a veterinarian come visit the class. Discuss varieties of animals and vaccinations. Remind the children that *veterinarian, visit, vaccination*, and *varieties* begin with the letter **V**.

Video Viewing Day

On a rainy or snowy afternoon, show the children some educational videos. Explain that *video* begins with the letter **V**. Be sure to have the children bring their favorite pillows for video viewing.

Volcano Fun

Use books, pictures, or videos to introduce the children to the term *volcano*. Tell the children that they can make their very own volcano in a bottle. To do this, give each child a small bottle with baking soda in it. Help each child pour some vinegar mixed with a little red food coloring into his or her bottle. Watch the lava overflow.

Snack Ideas

mixed raw vegetables, small vines of grapes, violet grape juice

---

Write a **V** on each vegetable.
Write an **F** on each fruit.

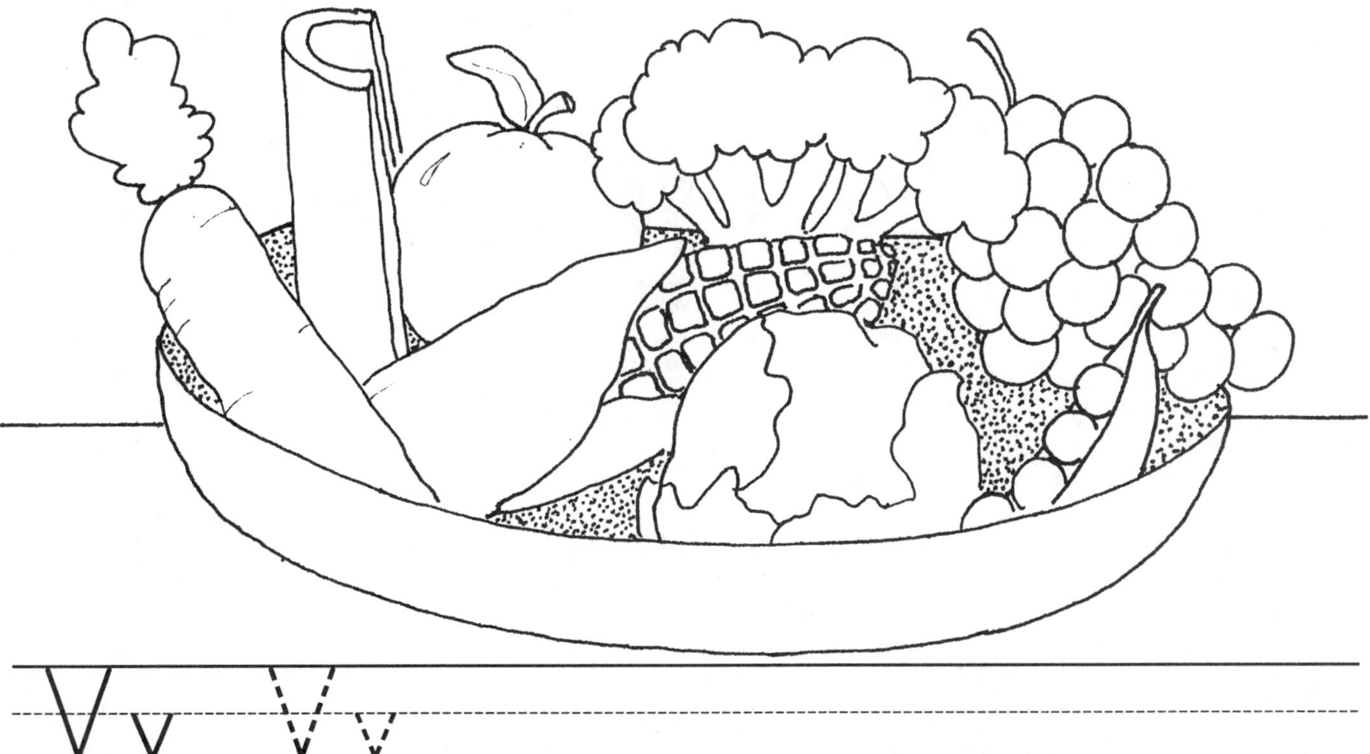

V v V v

Letter Practice
Tell the children that they are going to practice making uppercase and lowercase **W**'s on the chalkboard. Explain to them that they are going to be using paintbrushes dipped in water instead of chalk to make the letters. Have the children wash the chalkboards with sponges when they are finished making their letters.

Wishing Well
Place a miniature inflatable pool in the center of the classroom. Fill the pool with a little water. Ask the children to gather around the well. Tell them to think of a wish. Give each child a penny. Ask the children to toss their penny into the wishing well. Have them draw a picture of the wish they made. Help the children title their drawings "My Wishing Well Wish."

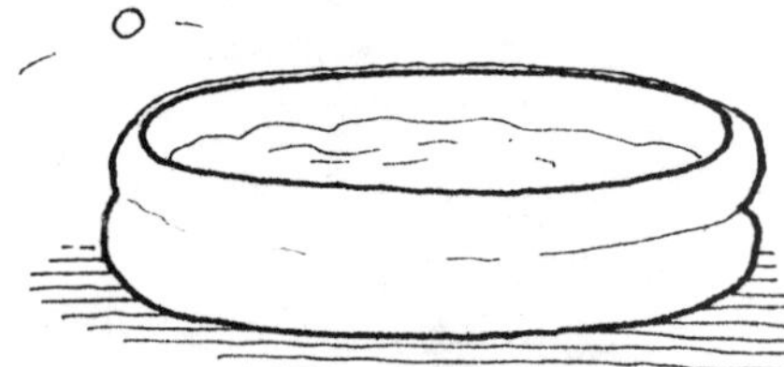

Winter Walks
Take the children on a walk on a winter day. Talk about the ways a winter walk is different from a summer walk. While on the walk, have the children wiggle, waddle, wave, and wink. Whisper to the children that *wiggle, waddle, wink, winter, walk, wave*, and *whisper* all begin with the letter **W**.

Worm World
Fill a clear plastic container with potting soil along with some decaying vegetation. Place a couple of worms in the container. Cover the top of the container but poke holes in the cover for air. In a couple of days, have the children examine the container noting the aspects of a worm's world.

Snack Ideas
watermelon, wheat crackers, water

Write the missing lines for each **W.**

W w W w

Aa•Bb•Cc•Dd•Ee•Ff•Gg•Hh•Ii•Jj•Kk•Ll•Mm•Nn•Oo•Pp•Qq•Rr•Ss•Tt•Uu•Vv•Ww•Xx•Yy•Zz

Letter Practice
Cut out tiny bone shapes from construction paper. Have the children glue the bones in the shape of an **X**. Explain that a doctor can see the bones inside a body when he or she takes an X-ray.

Xerox
Let each child make a Xerox of his or her hands on the Xerox machine. Then, have each child draw an uppercase and lowercase letter **X** in each hand.

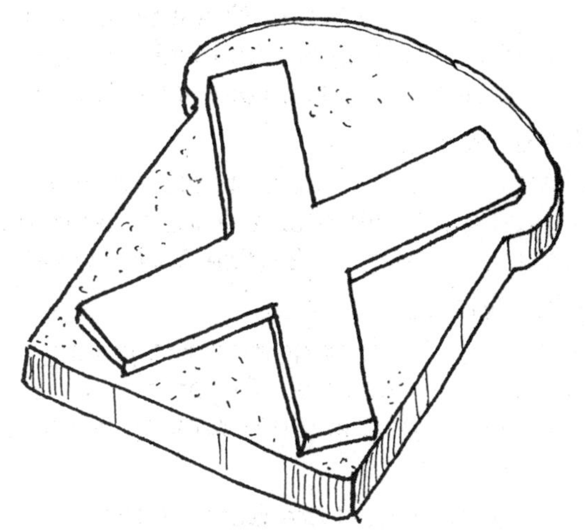

Xylophone Fun
Have the children take turns playing a xylophone. Explain how the **X** in xylophone is silent. Talk about the sound it makes.

X-ray Examination
See if a dentist, doctor, or veterinarian will provide the class with X-rays. Talk about different bones in people and animals. Talk about the advantages of having X-ray machines.

Snack Ideas
Make cheese sandwiches by having the children cut cheese slices into letter **X**'s. Have them place their cheese **X** on a sandwich.

Finish the words below by writing an **X**.

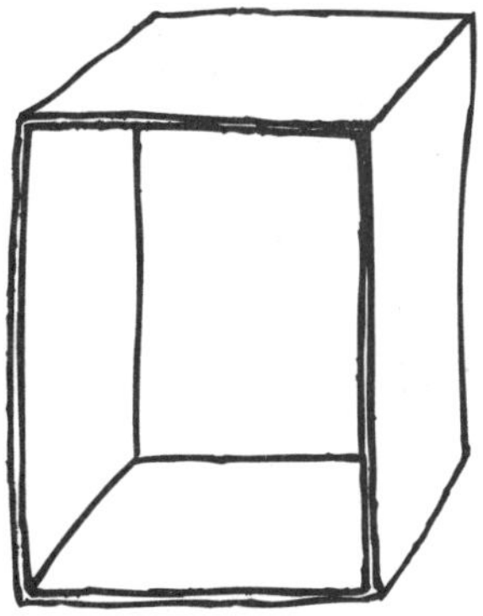

box

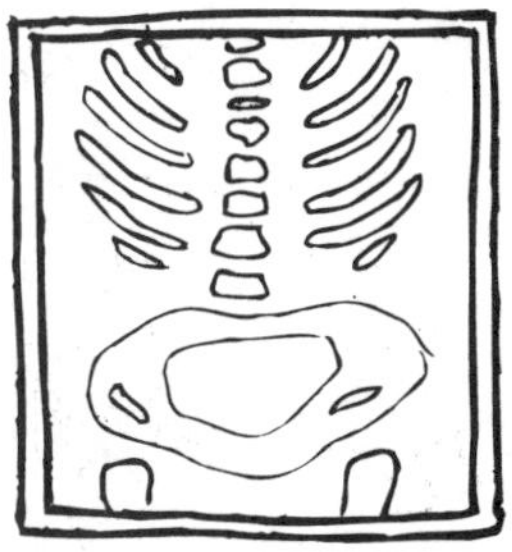

X-ray

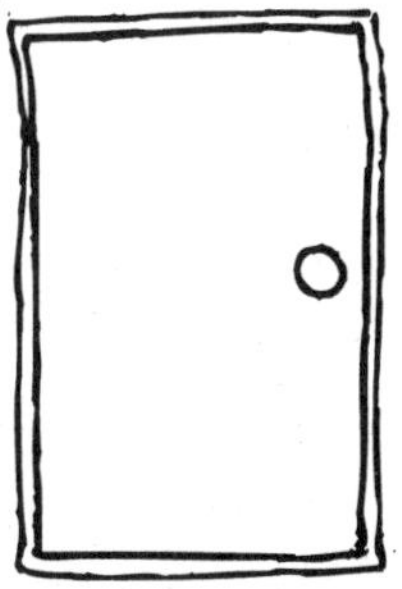

EXIT

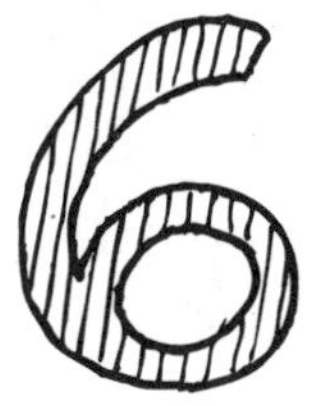

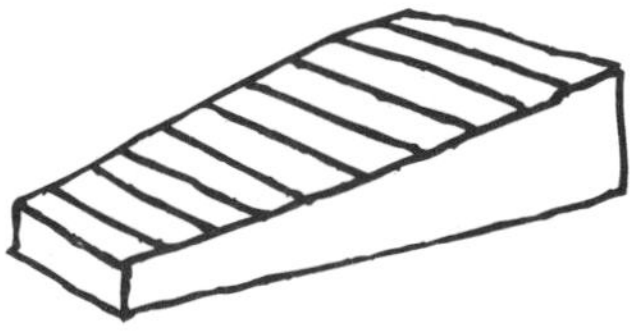

xylophone

six

Xx Xx

Aa • Bb • Cc • Dd • Ee • Ff • Gg • Hh • Ii • Jj • Kk • Ll • Mm • Nn • Oo • Pp • Qq • Rr • Ss • Tt • Uu • Vv • Ww • Xx • Yy • Zz

Letter Practice

Give each child a few strands of yellow yarn. Have the children practice making uppercase and lowercase **Y**'s on a piece of paper. Then have them glue their yarn to the letters they have written. Remind the children that *yarn* and *yellow* begin with the letter **Y**.

Yes/No

Give each child a paper plate. Have the children write the word *no* in the center of the plate. On the opposite side, have the children write the word *yes*. Help the children glue a tongue depressor to their plate. Tell the children that they should answer the questions you ask by holding their paper plate up with the correct answer facing you. Some questions you might ask include the following:

- Is a duck yellow?
- Are you young?
- Are you five years old yet?
- Do you like to play with yo-yos?
- Did you go to school yesterday?
- Do you think candy tastes yummy?

Yard Walk

Talk to the children about caring for a yard. Include cleaning, raking, mowing, and trimming. Explain how yard work is very difficult for elderly or sick people. Choose a day in the fall and have the children do yard work at school. Have them rake the leaves and pick up trash in an elderly or sick person's yard.

Snack Ideas

yogurt, yellow foods (bananas, corn, lemons, egg yolks), yams

---

How many lowercase **y**'s are there? ____

How many uppercase **Y**'s are there? ____

Yy Yy

Aa•Bb•Cc•Dd•Ee•Ff•Gg•Hh•Ii•Jj•Kk•Ll•Mm•Nn•Oo•Pp•Qq•Rr•Ss•Tt•Uu•Vv•Ww•Xx•Yy•Zz

Letter Practice

Supply the children with some zany colored paint. Have the children finger-paint uppercase and lowercase **Z**'s. Ask them to zip along as they paint the letter **Z**.

Zipper Practice

Divide the children into pairs. Give each pair a zipper. While one child holds the zipper top, the other child should try to unzip and re-zip the zipper. Have the children reverse roles and repeat the process.

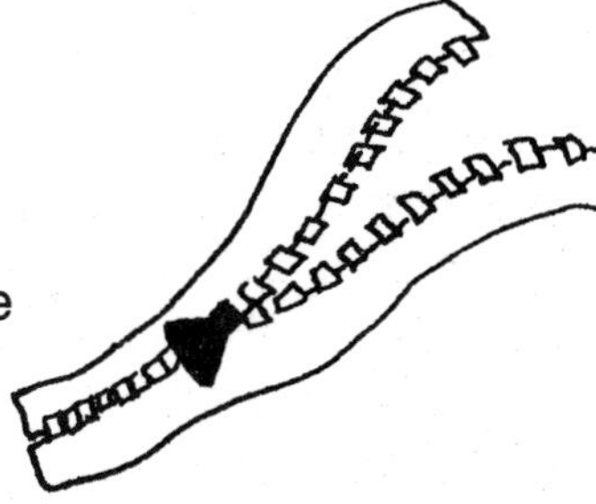

The Play Dough Zoo

Talk about zoo animals with the children. Ask them which animal they like the best and why. Have each child make a zoo animal out of play dough. When the children are finished, let them sort the animals.

Zucchini Art

Let the children watch you cut a zucchini in slices. Have them examine the slices. Provide paint and paper the children can use to make zucchini prints. Encourage overlapping and mixing colors. Have the children make Z shapes on their paper using the zucchinis.

Snack Ideas

zucchini slices, zoo animal crackers

Connect the dots to make the **Z**'s.

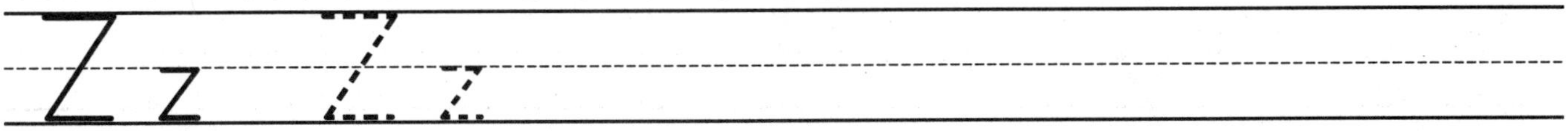

Z z

Front and Back Covers

For the teacher: Make a copy of this page for each child. Instruct the children to decorate each section to create front and back covers for their alphabet books.

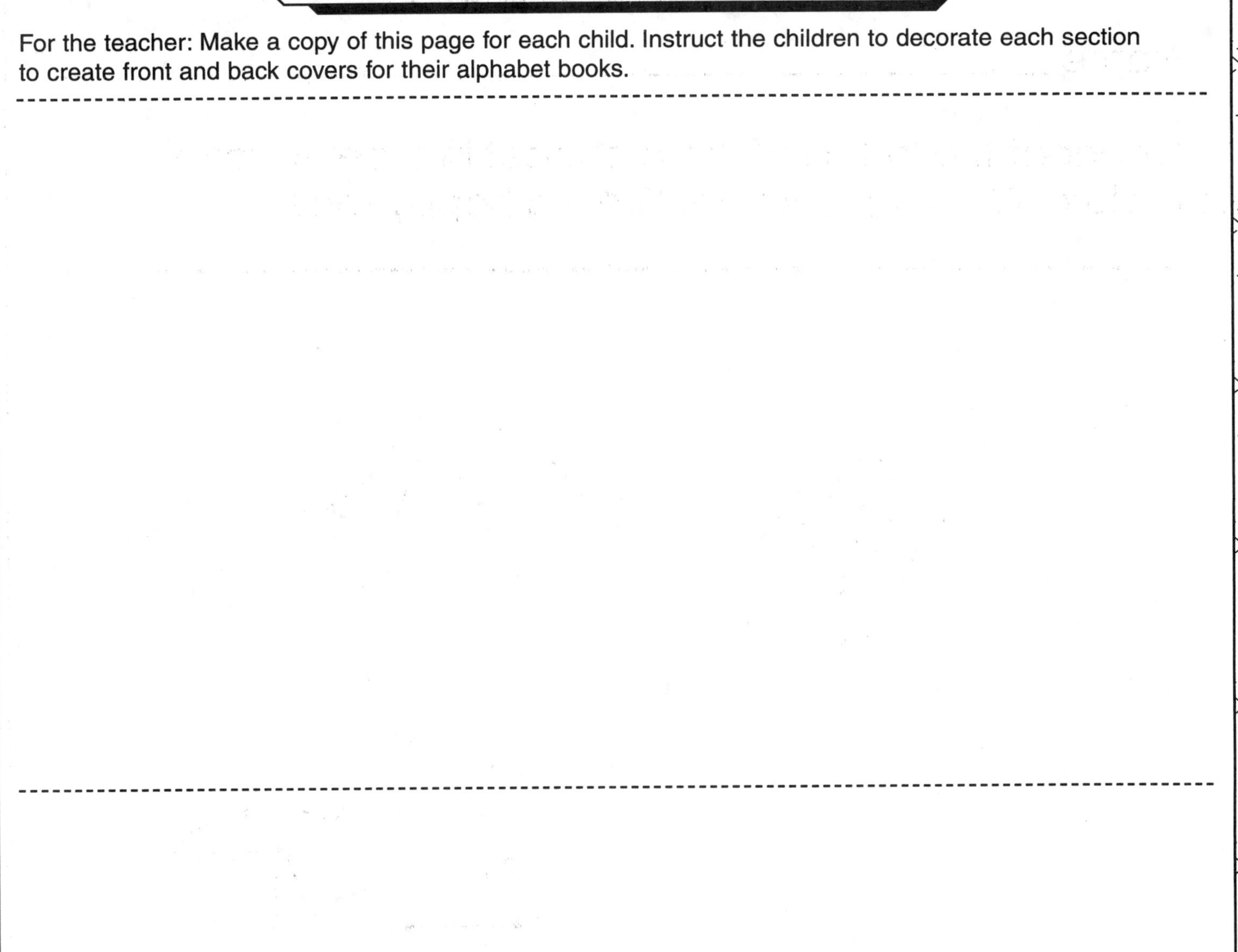

A Crazy Connection

Name ____

Connect the letters of the alphabet in order to form a picture. Color the picture. Draw a happy face.

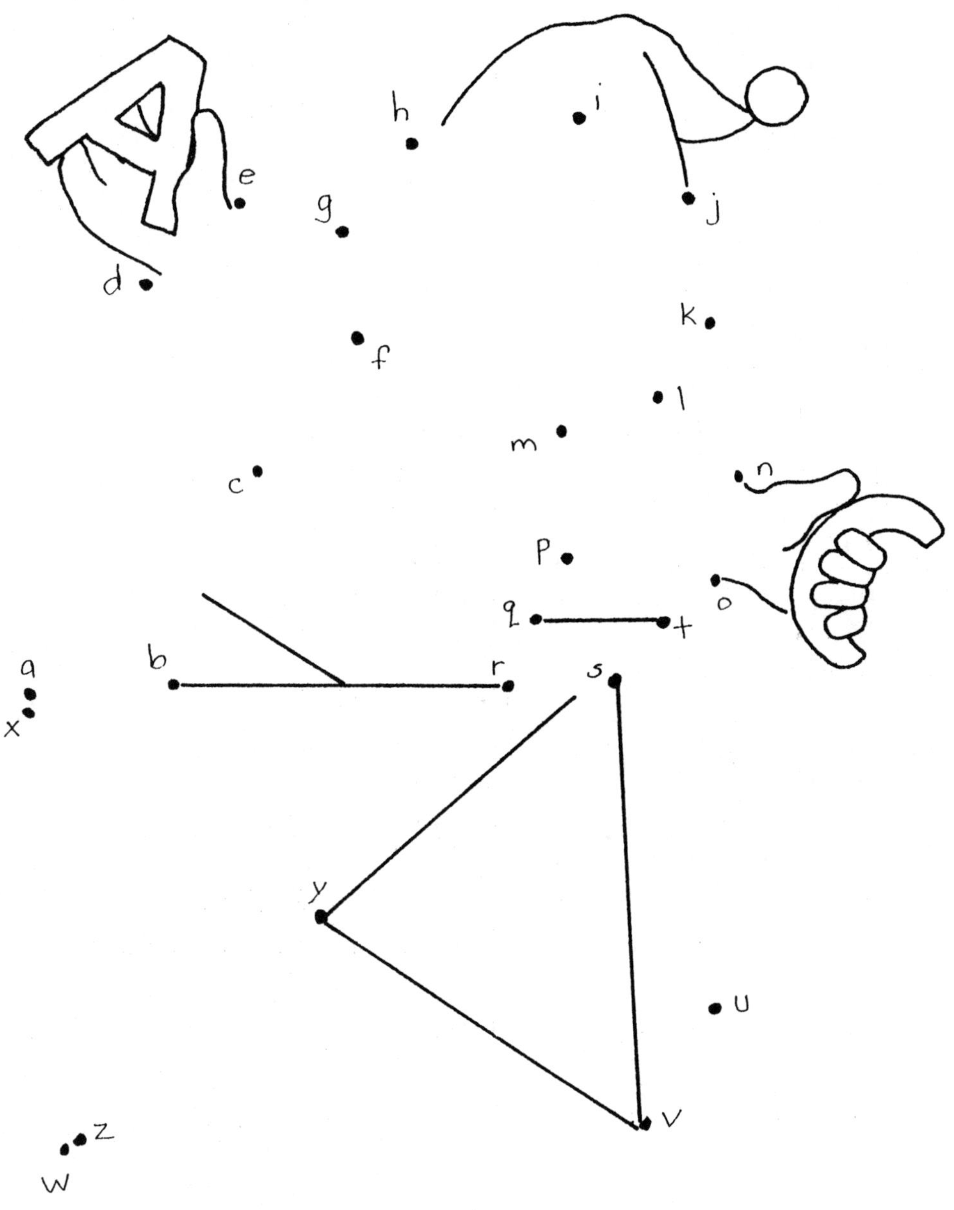

Looking for Letters

Name ________________________________

Find all the letters of the alphabet hidden in the picture below.

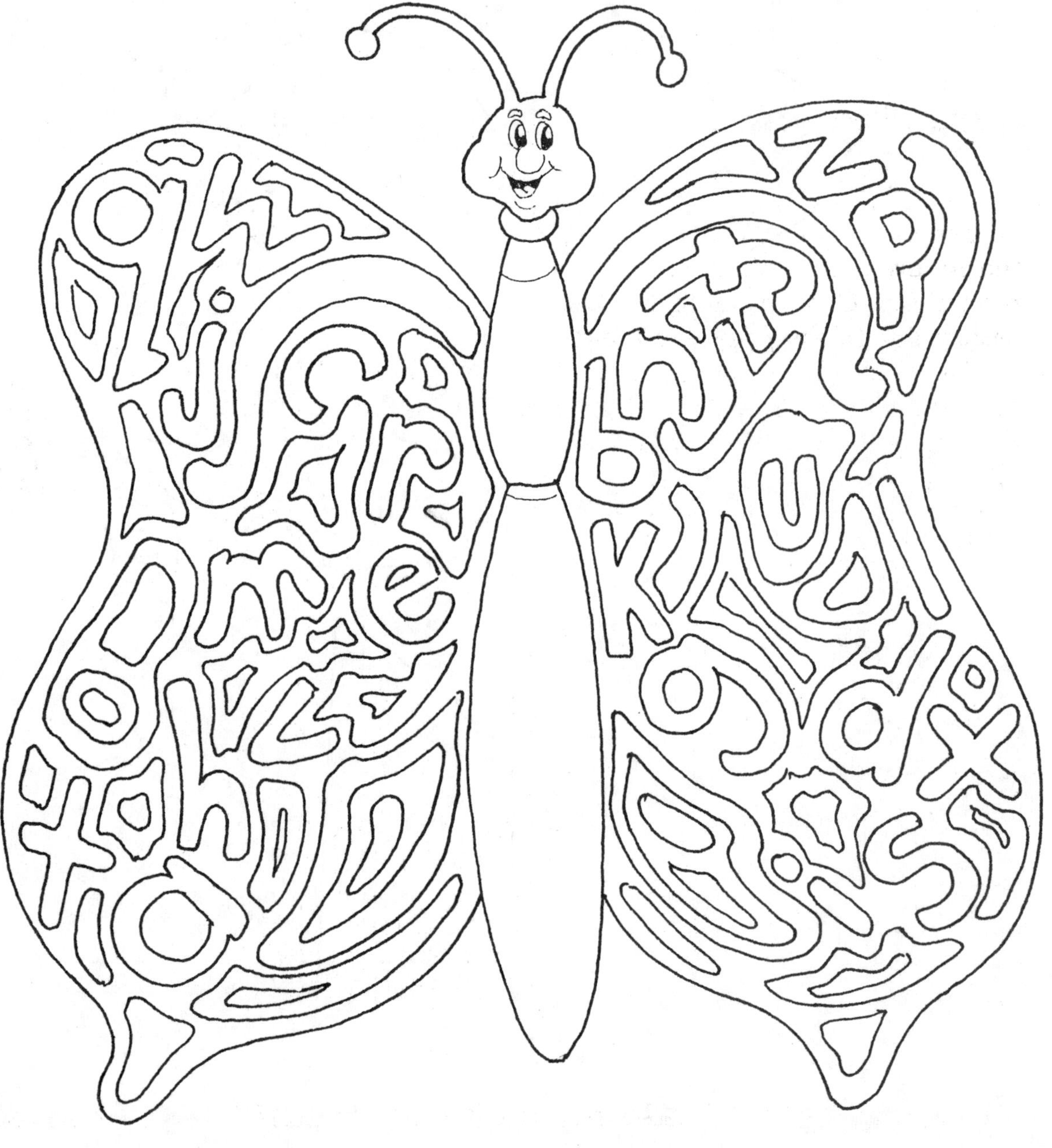